Best Easy D

Best Easy Day Hikes
Las Vegas

Bruce Grubbs

GUILFORD, CONNECTICUT
HELENA, MONTANA

AN IMPRINT OF GLOBE PEQUOT PRESS

FALCONGUIDES®

Copyright © 2010 by Morris Book Publishing, LLC

Layout: Kevin Mak
Project editor: John Burbidge
Maps by Bruce Grubbs © Morris Book Publishing, LLC

Library of Congress Cataloging-in-Publication Data
Grubbs, Bruce (Bruce O.)
 Best easy day hikes, Las Vegas / Bruce Grubbs.
    p. cm. – (Falconguides)
 ISBN 978-0-7627-5252-2
 1. Hiking–Nevada–Las Vegas Region–Guidebooks. 2. Trails–Nevada–
Las Vegas Region–Guidebooks. 3. Las Vegas Region (Nev.)–Guide-
books. I. Title.
 GV199.42.N32L374 2010
 917.93'135–dc22

                                                    2009029485

Printed in the United States of America
10 9 8 7 6 5 4 3 2 1

Contents

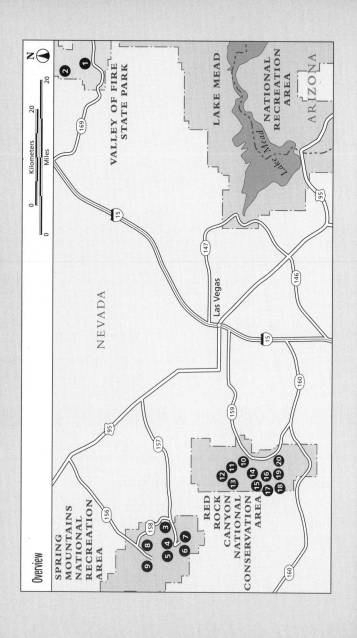

Acknowledgments

Special thanks to Don Bolton of Valley of Fire State Park for reviewing the manuscript. I would like to thank my many hiking companions down the years, who've put up with my incessant trail mapping and photography. Thanks to Duart Martin for her support and encouragement. And finally, thanks to my editors at Globe Pequot Press, Scott Adams and John Burbidge, for making a book out of my rough manuscript.

Introduction

When most people think of Las Vegas, they think of it as the entertainment center of the country. Not so well known is the fact that Las Vegas is also a hiker's paradise. Within an hour or so drive from the glitter and bright lights of casinos and hotels along The Strip are many fine hikes. This book details twenty of the easiest hikes that are readily accessible from the city. There are red rock desert hikes in the Valley of Fire and Red Rock Canyon National Recreation Area, while the lofty Spring Mountains feature alpine hikes that wander through ancient groves of bristlecone pines more than 2 miles above sea level.

The Las Vegas area is part of the basin and range geologic province, where long, relatively narrow mountain ranges are separated by wide valleys. It is also in the Mojave Desert, the lowest, hottest, and driest of the four North American deserts. The geologic forces that raised the mountains exposed a stunning variety of bedrock and created a dramatic landscape to explore. Elevations range from around 2,000 feet in Valley of Fire State Park to nearly 12,000 feet in the Spring Mountains. The creosote brush of the desert flats gives way to sagebrush, pinyon-pine and juniper woodland, open ponderosa pine stands, cool fir and aspen forest, ice-blasted bristlecone pines, and finally arctic tundra on the highest summits.

Millions of years ago, during the formation of the North American continent, the area that is now Nevada was stretched from east to west by crustal forces. Numerous north-tending fractures, or faults, formed as the rocks broke under the strain. Some of the resulting blocks sank to form

1

the valleys, while others rose to form the mountains. As the faulting continues to lower the basins and raise the mountains, erosion from water flowing downhill tends to wear down the mountains and fill the valleys. The topography we see today reflects the fact that the faulting is still active enough to keep the mountains from being worn down to a flat plain.

More recently, as these events go, a colder and wetter climate caused snow to accumulate in the higher ranges and form glaciers. The last of these glacial periods ended about 10,000 years ago but left its mark on the topography in the form of steep, glacially carved mountain peaks and classic U-shaped mountain valleys. As the climate warmed and the glaciers receded, the massive flow of meltwater collected in huge lakes rivaling the Great Lakes in size. In many parts of Nevada, the ancient shorelines of these lakes are clearly visible as terraces along the lower mountain slopes.

During the cooler glacial climate, extensive forests covered the valleys and bordered the lakes. As the last ice age gradually ended, the warming climate caused plants and animals to migrate up the mountainsides, following the upward movement of their preferred environment.

Hazards

Dehydration

Even in the mountains, where the summer air is cool, dehydration is a serious concern. Because the humidity is usually very low, your body loses moisture insensibly. Carry and drink plenty of water, and eat high-energy snacks for fuel and to help keep your electrolytes in balance. Both these measures are necessary to prevent heat exhaustion, which can develop into life-threatening sunstroke.

Plants and Animals

A few plants are hazardous to the touch, such as poison ivy and stinging nettle. Spiny plants like cactus are easy to avoid. Never eat any plant, unless you know what you are doing. Many common plants, especially mushrooms, are deadly.

Animals will leave you alone unless molested or provoked. Do not ever feed wild animals, as they rapidly get used to the handouts and then will vigorously defend their new food source. Around camp, problems with rodents can be avoided by hanging your food from rocks or trees. Even the toughest pack can be wrecked by a determined mouse or squirrel that has all night in which to work. Heavily used campsites present the worst problems, but in Nevada there's not much reason to camp in heavily used areas!

Rattlesnakes cause concern but can easily be avoided. They usually warn off intruders by rattling well before you reach striking range. Since rattlesnakes can strike no farther than half their body length, avoid placing your hands and feet in areas you cannot see, and walk several feet away from rock overhangs and shady ledges. Snakes prefer surfaces at about 80°F, so during hot weather they prefer the shade of bushes or rock overhangs, and in cool weather they will be found sunning themselves on open ground.

Weather

As a desert region, the weather in Las Vegas is stable for long periods. Even during the winter, when storms drop snow on the high peaks and rain on the desert floor, long periods of clear weather are the rule rather than the exception. Desert hiking is especially fine during the winter, when the mountaintops are buried in snow. Spring and fall are normally dry and offer the best weather for hiking at all elevations. After wet winters, spring often brings fantastic displays of wildflowers to the desert. When the heat of summer blasts the desert, it is best to either hike early in the morning or retreat to the alpine trails of the Spring Mountains. Late summer brings a second wet period, the North American Monsoon, an influx of seasonal moisture from the Gulf of Mexico. Later summer mornings usually dawn clear, but by noon towering cumulus clouds often form over the mountains and develop into massive thunderstorms. Plan summer hikes to be off exposed ridges and summits by noon to avoid the thunderstorm hazards of lightning, high wind, and hail.

The best source for up-to-date weather information is the National Weather Service in Las Vegas; their Web site is www.weather.gov/lasvegas. Commercial weather sources concentrate on urban areas and highway corridors, but by using the National Weather Service Web site, you can click on a map and get a specific point forecast for the trail you plan to hike. This is important because the weather in the mountains is usually much different from the weather in the city.

Gear Every Hiker Should Carry

- Water
- Food
- Sun hat
- Sunscreen
- Sunglasses
- Durable hiking shoes or boots
- Synthetic fleece jacket or pullover
- Rain gear
- Map

- Compass
- First-aid kit
- Signal mirror
- Toilet paper and zippered plastic bag

Environmental Considerations

The desert is a fragile environment that deserves our utmost care and respect. Please adhere to some simple practices when hiking and camping in the desert.

Stay on the trail. Don't cut switchbacks. It takes more effort and increases erosion.

Be careful with fires. Smokers should stop at a bare spot or rock ledge, then make certain that all smoking materials are out before continuing. Due to fire hazard, it may be illegal to smoke while traveling. Never smoke or light any kind of fire on windy days or when the fire danger is high, because wildfires can start easily and spread explosively.

Control your pet. Although dogs are allowed in all the areas covered by this book, it is your responsibility to keep them from barking and bothering wildlife or other hikers. In national forests, dogs must be kept under control and on a leash when required.

Respect the environment. Don't cut live trees or plants of any kind, carve on trees or rocks, pick wildflowers, or build structures such as rock campfire rings.

Share the trail. Many of the trails in this book are open to horseback riders as well as hikers, and some are open to mountain bikers as well. Horses always have the right-of-way over hikers and cyclists, both of which should move off the trail downhill and remain still until the horses have passed. Talking quietly to the riders helps convince the horses that you are a person and not some weird monster with a hump on its back. Don't make sudden movements or noises.

Technically, hikers have the right-of-way over cyclists, but in practice it's more reasonable for hikers to step off the trail so as to avoid forcing the riders off trail. On their part, cyclists should be courteous, always ride under control, and warn hikers of their approach.

Sanitation

A short walk in any popular recreation area will show you that few people seem to know how to answer the call of nature away from facilities. Diseases such as Giardiasis are spread by poor human sanitation. If facilities are available, use them. In the backcountry, select a site at least 100 yards from streams, lakes, springs, and dry washes. Avoid barren, sandy soil, if possible. Next, dig a small "cat-hole" about 6 inches down into the organic layer of the soil. (Some people carry a small plastic trowel for this purpose.) When finished, refill the hole, covering any toilet paper. In some areas, regulations require that you carry out used toilet paper, and the principles of Leave No Trace suggest you always carry it out.

As far as trash goes, if you carried it in, you can also carry it out. Do not bury food or trash. Animals will dig it up. Never feed wild creatures. They become dependent on human food, which can lead to unpleasant encounters and cause the animal to starve during the off-season.

Three Falcon Zero-Impact Principles
- Leave with everything you brought.
- Leave no sign of your visit.
- Leave the landscape as you found it.

How to Use This Book

This book is broken into three sections, covering Valley of Fire State Park, Spring Mountains National Recreation Area, and the Red Rock Canyon National Conservation Area. Valley of Fire State Park is northeast of Las Vegas and east of I-15. The Spring Mountains are a long, narrow mountain range located west and northwest of the city, and the Red Rock Canyon National Conservation Area lies along the Sandstone Bluffs at the south end of the Spring Mountains. All three areas offer fine hiking. The shortest hikes are in the Valley of Fire, while the longest and highest elevation hikes are in the northern Spring Mountains, in the Spring Mountains National Recreation Area. The greatest concentration of hiking trails in the Las Vegas area is within the Red Rock National Conservation Area.

Using the Trail Descriptions

Each hike in the book has a number and name. Some trails have more than one common name, and other hikes use more than one trail to complete a loop or otherwise create a more interesting route. In each case, I've attempted to name the hike for the best-known trail or feature. Each hike starts with a general description of the highlights and attractions. A summary of the hike follows, with at-a-glance information.

Distance: This is the total mileage of the hike. For out-and-back hikes, it includes the return mileage. Loop hikes include the total distance around the loop. Some loops may have an out-and-back section, or cherry stem. I've selected hikes that do not require a car shuttle, for simplicity and so that you can spend more of your hiking time on the trail instead of in a car. Distances were measured on digital topographic maps and may vary slightly from official mileages but are consistent through the book.

Approximate hiking time: This is based on an average hiker who is reasonably fit. More casual hikers should allow more time. The hiking time does not include time for lunch stops, wildlife view stops, photography, or other distractions. Plan on more time for such activities. Groups should remember that the party travels at the speed of the slowest member.

Difficulty: All hikes in this book are rated easy or moderate. There are no strenuous or difficult hikes in the book, but sections of trails may be steep, rough, or otherwise more strenuous than the overall rating would indicate. Just about anyone should be able to do an easy hike. Moderate hikes require a bit of fitness, and beginners should allow extra time.

Trail surface: The type of tread you'll be walking on.

Best season: This indicates the best season to do a particular hike. Low-elevation hikes in the Valley of Fire and the Red Rocks are generally best hiked from fall through spring because of the extremely hot summers. During the summer, higher-elevation hikes in the Spring Mountains are preferable. If you hike at low elevation during the summer, get an early start and take plenty of water.

Water availability: Although day hikers should carry all the water they need, this section lists known water sources for emergency use. All water should be purified before use.

Other trail users: These may include equestrians and mountain bikers.

Canine compatibility: If dogs are allowed, they must be on a leash. In Valley of Fire State Park, dogs must be on a leash no longer than 6 feet. This is just common courtesy to other hikers, some of whom may have had bad experiences with dogs. If your dog barks or runs up to other hikers, even in a friendly way, you are giving dog owners a bad name. Also, clean up after your dog.

Fees and permits: Entrance fees and permits required, if any, are listed here. Valley of Fire State Park (a Nevada state park) and the Red Rock Canyon National Conservation Area (administered by the Bureau of Land Management) charge entrance fees. At present, Spring Mountains National Recreation Area (administered by the U.S. Forest Service) does not, but this could change in the future.

Maps: Each hike has a map showing the trail and any pertinent landmarks. Hikers wishing to explore further, or off trail, should carry the U.S. Geological Survey topographic maps as listed here. These are the most detailed maps for terrain and natural features but do not show all trails.

Trail contacts: This section lists the name, address, phone, and Web site of the managing agency. It's a good idea to contact the agency for up-to-date trail information before your hike.

Finding the trailhead: GPS coordinates in UTM are given for all trailheads. Make sure your GPS is set to the WGS84 datum. Trailhead driving directions are given from Las Vegas.

The hike: This is a narrative description of the hike route and attractions you'll find along the way. There are also descriptions of relevant natural or human history.

Miles and directions: This table lists the key points, such as trail intersections, or turning points on a cross-country hike, by miles and tenths. You should be able to find the route with this table alone. The mileages in this book do not necessarily agree with distances found on trails signs, agency mileages, and other descriptions because trail miles are measured by a variety of methods and personnel. All mileages in this book were carefully measured using digital topographic mapping software for accuracy and consistency.

Trail Finder

Best Hikes for Geology Lovers

Best Hikes for Children

Best Hikes for Dogs

Best Hikes for Great Views

Best Hikes for Photographers

Best Hikes for Canyons

Best Hikes for Nature Lovers

Map Legend

15	Interstate Highway
97	U.S. Highway
156	State Highway
57A	Local/County Road
= = = = = = =	Unpaved Road
▬▬▬▬▬▬	Featured Route
- - - - - - -	Trail
....	Other Route
- .. - .. - .. -	State Line
⌇⌇⌇⌇	Intermittent Stream
⬭	Lake/Pond
⬓	State Park
⬓	National Recreation Area
✕	Mine
🖼	Nature Trail
P	Parking
)(	Pass
▲	Peak
🍴	Picnic Area
■	Point of Interest/Structure
⛷	Ski Area
ρ	Spring
○	Town
11	Trailhead
?	Viewpoint/Overlook
🔷	Visitor Center
≩	Waterfall

Valley of Fire State Park

This small unit of the Nevada State Park system is located northeast of Las Vegas and is reached via I-15. The park gets its name from the red sandstone formations found in the park. The dome-shaped formations are often referred to as "slickrock." Up close, sandstone is anything but slick, so the term probably relates to the rounded shapes carved out of the soft rock by the forces of erosion. Other sedimentary rock, including shale and limestone, contribute their own colors and shapes to this desert landscape. The landscape is so unique that a number of movies have been shot here.

Evidence of prehistoric people is found in the park in the form of rock art decorating several sites. The main period of occupation, by the Basketmaker and Anasazi Cultures, appears to have been from 300 B.C. to A.D. 1150. Because of the dry desert climate and the general lack of reliable surface water, most native use was probably transitory. Remember that all artifacts are protected by law and should not be disturbed.

Spring and fall are the ideal times to visit Valley of Fire. The weather is generally stable and mild. Winter is not a bad time, as snow is rare in the park. Summers are hot and hiking is best done early in the day.

The park has several picnic areas, for those who want to relax at a shaded facility before or after their hike. The park also has two campgrounds, which are first come, first served. There are also a number of points of interest accessible from the park road, including the petroglyphs at Atlatl Rock, the Beehives formations, the old CCC cabins, the Clark Memorial honoring a pioneer traveler, the Petrified Logs, Rainbow Vista, and the Seven Sisters formations.

1 Mouses Tank

A day hike on an interpretive trail in Valley of Fire State Park, this short walk features petrified sand dunes, prehistoric petroglyphs, and natural water tanks.

Distance: 0.8 mile out and back
Approximate hiking time: 1 hour
Difficulty: Easy
Trail surface: Dirt and rocks
Best season: Fall through spring
Water availability: None
Other trail users: None
Canine compatibility: Dogs allowed, on leashes 6 feet in length or less

Fees and permits: Entrance fee
Maps: USGS: Valley of Fire East, Valley of Fire West
Trail contacts: Valley of Fire State Park, P.O. Box 515, Overton, NV 89040; (702) 397-2088; http://parks.nv.gov/vf.htm
Special considerations: During the summer, hike early in the day and carry plenty of water.

Finding the trailhead: From Las Vegas, drive northeast on I-15 approximately 55 miles, then turn right onto NV 169, which is signed for Valley of Fire State Park. Continue into the park, and turn left at the Visitor Center, approximately 18 miles from I-15. After 0.2 mile, turn left (before reaching the Visitor Center), and continue about 1 mile to the signed Mouses Tank parking area on the right. GPS: UTM 11S 722565E 4035743N

The Hike

The trail follows Petroglyph Canyon east from the parking area. Brochures are available at the trailhead explaining various features along this short walk. It points out a couple of petroglyphs along the way, but sharp-eyed hikers will see several more. After a relatively straight section, the wash

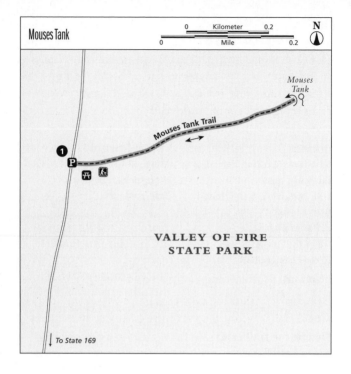

To State 169

veers sharply left and, in a few dozen yards, drops into the first of several natural water tanks. This water may seem stagnant and uninviting (and is not currently safe to drink), but it would become infinitely more valuable if one was on foot many miles from civilization.

In 1897 Mouse, a Paiute Indian who was suspected of several crimes, hid out in the intricate Valley of Fire area to avoid capture. He used this water tank and probably others to survive in this nearly waterless area.

The striking red rocks of the Valley of Fire are Aztec sandstone, which is composed of petrified sand dunes. Tiny grains of windblown sand make up the rock, and the sloping surfaces of the ancient sand dunes are clearly visible in the rock faces along the trail. The forces of erosion, primarily that of water, have acted over millions of years to sculpt the soft rock into the weird shapes found in the park.

In the backcountry, the hiker will encounter artifacts of various ages. Some of these structures, tools, and other artifacts date from before European discovery of the Americas. Others were built by early settlers and explorers. All are valuable links with our history and prehistory. Yet increasingly this evidence of early civilization is being destroyed by vandals. Federal and state laws have been passed to protect such antiquities, but ultimately the responsibility must lie with the users of the backcountry. Keep in mind that the relationships between artifacts in a site are often more important than the artifacts themselves. Petroglyphs and pictographs (rock drawings) have lasted thousands of years but are easily destroyed by thoughtless people.

Miles and Directions

0.0 Leave Mouses Tank Trailhead and follow Mouses Tank Trail east.

0.3 The trail and the wash veer sharply left.

0.4 You'll reach Mouses Tank, the destination for the hike; return the way you came.

0.8 Arrive back at Mouses Tank Trailhead.

2 White Domes

This loop hike takes you through the White Domes area in the primitive and less-traveled northern area of the park, featuring sandstone formations with brilliant and contrasting colors.

Distance: 1.5-mile loop
Approximate hiking time: 1 hour
Difficulty: Easy
Trail surface: Dirt and rocks
Best season: Fall through spring
Water availability: None
Other trail users: None
Canine compatibility: Dogs allowed, on leashes 6 feet in length or less

Fees and permits: Entrance fee
Maps: USGS: Valley of Fire East, Valley of Fire West
Trail contacts: Valley of Fire State Park, P.O. Box 515, Overton, NV 89040; (702) 397-2088; http://parks.nv.gov/vf.htm
Special considerations: During the summer, hike early in the day and carry plenty of water.

Finding the trailhead: From Las Vegas, drive northeast on I-15 approximately 55 miles, then turn right onto NV 169, which is signed for Valley of Fire State Park. Continue into the park, and turn left at the Visitor Center, approximately 18 miles from I-15. After 0.2 mile, turn left (before reaching the Visitor Center), and continue about 1.6 miles to a junction. Keep left, and continue to the end of the road at the White Domes parking area. GPS: UTM 11S 720925E 4041132N

The Hike

The trail loops through the colorful sandstone "slickrock" formations in the White Domes area.

Note the nearly white sandstone in this area, in contrast to the deep red sandstone near the Visitor Center. The color

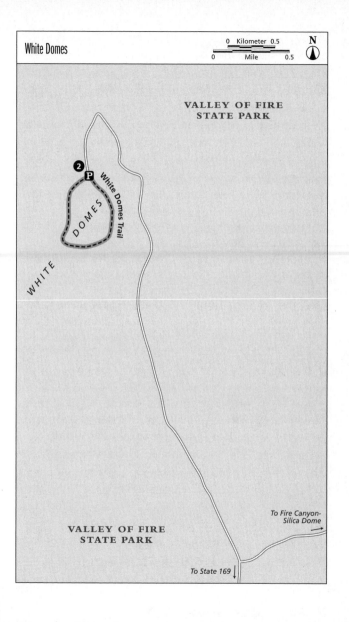

in the rock is caused by traces of iron minerals that have oxidized, or literally rusted. Subtle changes in the colors, from white to tan, purple, maroon, and red, are thought to be caused by underground water movement, which leached the oxidized iron.

The Muddy Mountains are made up of limestone, which is much older than the sandstone in the Valley of Fire. Normally younger rocks are found on top of older rocks, because the layers are deposited in sequence. But here the older limestone was once on top of the sandstone. This was caused by thrust faulting during the building of the North American continent, in which the limestone was forced many miles over the top of the sandstone.

The Virgin Mountains on the Arizona-Nevada state line are visible 30 miles to the northeast. These 8,000-foot mountains often have snow during the winter. Forty miles to the northwest, the 10,000-foot Sheep Creek Range dominates the distant skyline, with the White Domes area forming the middle distance. To the south, the domes and canyons of Fire Canyon shade from white to red, with the somber gray tones of the Muddy Mountains forming the skyline about 5 miles away.

Many believe that wind erodes desert landscapes such as this one. However, wind plays a minor part, mainly moving loose sand and heaping it into small sand dunes. Water is actually responsible for most of the landforms within the park. That seems fantastic in this arid landscape, especially if one has only seen the rare and gentle winter rains. But every few years the area is subjected to heavy rains from strong summer thunderstorms and, even more rarely, prolonged winter rain like the two-week rain of January 1993. The power of water becomes more apparent when one multiplies the effects of one of these storms by millions of storms occurring over many millions of years.

Miles and Directions

0.0 Leave the White Domes Trailhead and hike in either direction on the loop.

1.5 Return to White Domes Trailhead.

Spring Mountains

The Spring Mountains lie west and northwest of Las Vegas and rise to 11,811 feet at Mount Charleston. This popular recreational area features a ski area, summer homes, and plenty of trails for the hiker. Much of the Spring Mountains, including all the hikes in this book, are now part of the Spring Mountains National Recreation Area, which is administered by the U.S. Forest Service.

Because of their high elevation, the Spring Mountains are the summer hiking destination of choice for Las Vegas-based hikers. Access is easy via US 95 and two state highways that lead to trailheads in Kyle and Lee Canyons on the east side of the range.

Winters can be long and serious on the high ridges of the Spring Mountains, which doesn't provide good conditions for hiking. Lower elevations can be hiked during the spring, but the highest elevations may have significant snow cover into June. Summer and fall are the best times to explore these mountains, and the weather is delightful. Although late summer does bring the North American Monsoon, this seasonal influx of moisture usually causes brief afternoon thundershowers that dissipate after sunset. Hikers should stay off high ridges and peaks during afternoons when thunderstorms are building. Mornings are almost always clear and cool and can be downright cold, even in midsummer, on the highest ridges. Fall weather is generally clear and cool, and the fine weather is complemented by the slashes of bright fall color that grace the mountainsides. One caution: Though the air is usually cool in the Spring Mountains, it is also very dry, which means that your body loses a great deal of moisture as insensible sweat. Be sure to carry and drink plenty of water, and eat nutritious snacks to maintain both hydration and electrolyte balance.

Massive limestone cliffs are a distinctive feature of the Spring Mountains. Deposited in the depths of an ancient ocean by a steady rain of the microscopic shells of tiny sea animals, the layers were then buried under thousands of feet of additional sediments, and then compressed into the hard gray rock you see today. Tectonic, mountain-building forces at the western margin of the North American continent then stretched the earth's crust in the Nevada region, causing the rocks to break apart into blocks. Some blocks sank to form valleys, and other blocks rose to form mountains such as the Spring Mountains. Erosion from water, snow, and ice then carved the mountains in the shapes you see today, a process that continues.

3 Fletcher Canyon

This is an easy hike up a canyon in the Spring Mountains to a spring. Those who wish a longer, harder hike can continue up the canyon above the spring, using an informal trail.

Distance: 2.0 miles out and back
Approximate hiking time: 2 hours
Difficulty: Easy
Trail surface: Dirt and rocks
Best season: Spring through fall
Water availability: None
Other trail users: Equestrians
Canine compatibility: Dogs allowed on leashes
Fees and permits: None
Maps: USGS: Charleston Peak

Trail contacts: Spring Mountains National Recreation Area, Humboldt-Toiyabe National Forest, 4701 N. Torrey Pines Dr., Las Vegas 89130-2301; (702) 515-5400; www.fs.fed.us/r4/htnf/districts/smnra
Special considerations: Although the air is cool at these high elevations, it is dry and you may not realize how much moisture you are losing. Carry and drink plenty of water, and use a good sunscreen.

Finding the trailhead: From Las Vegas, drive approximately 15 miles northwest on US 95, and then turn left onto NV 157 (Kyle Canyon Road). Continue 18 miles to the trailhead on the right. There is additional parking on the left side of the highway. GPS: UTM 11S 624849E 4014147N

The Hike

The trail climbs gradually up the canyon, following a wash with occasional seasonal water, through open stands of ponderosa pine, pinyon pine, mountain mahogany, and manzanita. The maintained trail ends at a small spring, which is

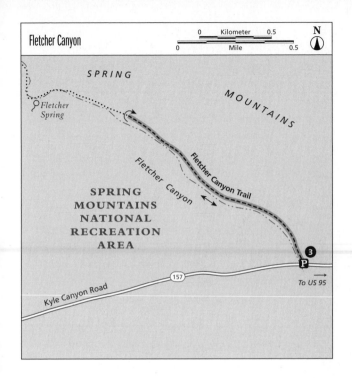

SPRING MOUNTAINS

MOUNTAINS

Fletcher Spring

Fletcher Canyon Trail

Fletcher Canyon

SPRING MOUNTAINS NATIONAL RECREATION AREA

3

P

To US 95

157

Kyle Canyon Road

the turnaround point. It is possible to continue up Fletcher Canyon using an informal trail into a narrow slot canyon. This will require some rock scrambling.

Manzanita, which means "little apple" in Spanish, is an evergreen shrub with distinctive, curly red bark and stiff, twisting branches. It is one of the common components of chaparral, the brushy mix that covers vast areas at intermediate elevations in the American west.

Chaparral, also sometimes called "mountain brush habitat," is a mix of shrubs that cover entire mountainsides between 5,000 and 9,000 feet. Gambel oak, cliffrose, manzanita, sagebrush, chokecherry, and mountain mahogany are common components of chaparral. Although heavy patches of chaparral can be difficult to hike through, the low brush provides excellent cover for wildlife. Chaparral is extremely fire-prone, especially during dry summers, and brushy hillsides burn with intensity and the fire spreads quickly. Usually the roots survive even the hottest fires, and the brush regenerates quickly after a burn.

Miles and Directions

0.0 Leave the Fletcher Canyon Trailhead on the Fletcher Canyon Trail.

1.0 Arrive at an unnamed spring, the destination for the hike; return the way you came.

2.0 Arrive back at Fletcher Canyon Trailhead.

4 Mary Jane Falls

This is a popular route to a cascading waterfall, located in the head of spectacular Kyle Canyon. It also offers views of Big Falls. The waterfalls flow all year but are at their best during spring after a snowy winter.

Distance: 2.4 miles out and back
Approximate hiking time: 2 hours
Difficulty: Easy
Trail surface: Dirt and rocks
Best season: Spring through fall
Water availability: None
Other trail users: Equestrians
Canine compatibility: Dogs allowed on leashes
Fees and permits: None
Maps: USGS: Charleston Peak

Trail contacts: Spring Mountains National Recreation Area, Humboldt-Toiyabe National Forest, 4701 N. Torrey Pines Dr., Las Vegas 89130-2301; (702) 515-5400; www.fs.fed.us/r4/htnf/districts/smnra
Special considerations: Although the air is cool at these high elevations, it is dry and you may not realize how much moisture you are losing. Carry and drink plenty of water, and use a good sunscreen.

Finding the trailhead: From Las Vegas, drive approximately 15 miles northwest on US 95, and then turn left onto NV 157 (Kyle Canyon Road). Continue 20.7 miles, then bear right onto Echo Canyon Road (NV 157 turns sharply left). Go 0.4 mile, then turn left onto a gravel road, which ends at the trailhead after 0.2 mile. GPS: UTM 11S 620495E 4014297N

The Hike

The popular Mary Jane Falls Trail starts out as a gradual ascent through fine stands of ponderosa pine, white fir,

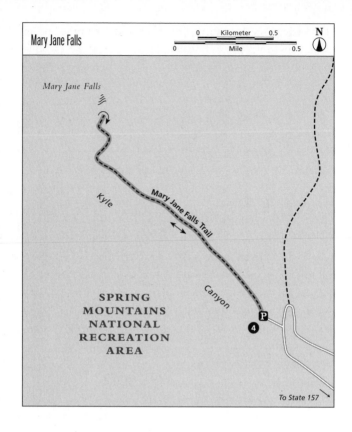

Mary Jane Falls

Kyle

Mary Jane Falls Trail

Canyon

SPRING
MOUNTAINS
NATIONAL
RECREATION
AREA

To State 157

mountain mahogany, and quaking aspen. Smaller, scruffy-looking mountain mahogany is also present. As the trail nears the head of the canyon, it starts to climb more steeply in a series of short switchbacks. The trail ends at the base of the falls, which cascade down the steep cliffs. The falls are at their best during early spring, after snowmelt. At this time of the year, you may also see Big Falls a mile to the south. Charleston Peak is visible to the west.

Massive limestone formations such as those in the Spring Mountains are commonly riddled with caves. The carbonate rocks that make up limestone are easily dissolved by groundwater moving along faults and joints and other flaws in the rock, creating cavities that sometimes become large caves. In the Spring Mountains, groundwater appears at the surface as the numerous springs that give the range its name.

Mountain mahogany is a plant that is common at higher altitudes on Nevada mountain ranges. It grows as a shrub or a small tree, favoring arid, rocky, gravelly slopes with maximum sun exposure. Mountain mahogany often has several trunks and grows in a contorted shape, which definitely adds to the wild and exposed mood of the places it is usually found. Native people used the wood for bows, spears, and digging sticks. They also boiled the bark with Mormon tea stems to create a tea used for medicinal purposes. Mountain mahogany also provides good forage and cover for wildlife.

Miles and Directions

0.0 Leave Mary Jane Falls Trailhead and follow the Mary Jane Falls Trail westward.

1.2 Arrive at the base of Mary Jane Falls, the destination for the hike; now, return the way you came.

2.4 Arrive back at Mary Jane Falls Trailhead.

5 Trail Canyon

This scenic hike climbs up a canyon through impressive limestone cliffs to a saddle and viewpoint.

Distance: 3.6 miles out and back

Approximate hiking time: 5 hours

Difficulty: Moderate due to elevation gain

Trail surface: Dirt and rocks

Best season: Spring through fall

Water availability: None

Other trail users: Equestrians

Canine compatibility: Dogs allowed on leashes

Fees and permits: None

Maps: USGS: Charleston Peak

Trail contacts: Spring Mountains National Recreation Area, Humboldt-Toiyabe National Forest, 4701 N. Torrey Pines Dr., Las Vegas 89130-2301; (702) 515-5400; www.fs.fed.us/r4/htnf/districts/smnra

Special considerations: Although the air is cool at these high elevations, it is dry and you may not realize how much moisture you are losing. Carry and drink plenty of water, and use a good sunscreen.

Finding the trailhead: From Las Vegas, drive approximately 15 miles northwest on US 95, and then turn left onto NV 157 (Kyle Canyon Road). Continue 20.7 miles, then bear right onto Echo Canyon Road (NV 157 turns sharply left). Go 0.5 mile, where the road makes a sharp right and becomes Crestview Dr. The trailhead is on the left side of the curve. GPS: UTM 11S 620574E 4014439N

The Hike

A steady climb through open stands of ponderosa pine and quaking aspen leads to the junction with the North Loop Trail at a saddle on Cockscomb Ridge. As you ascend, you'll have good views of the massive limestone

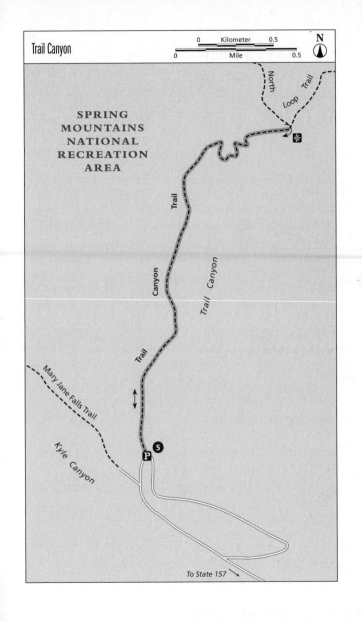

Trail Canyon

0   Kilometer   0.5
0   Mile   0.5

N

SPRING
MOUNTAINS
NATIONAL
RECREATION
AREA

North

Loop Trail

Trail

Canyon

Trail Canyon

Trail

Mary Jane Falls Trail

Kyle Canyon

P 5

To State 157

cliffs in Kyle Canyon. The saddle offers sweeping views of the Spring Mountains and Mount Charleston and is the turnaround point for this hike. The trail to the left continues to the summit of Mount Charleston, a long, strenuous hike. For details, see my other FalconGuide, *Hiking Nevada*.

Quaking aspen is the most widespread tree in North America. It grows at higher elevations in the mountains of Nevada, favoring cooler, north-facing slopes as well as sheltered canyon bottoms. The tall, graceful trees are about 1 foot in diameter and reach about 50 to 70 feet in height. The smooth, white bark makes a vivid contrast to the associated evergreen trees. The leaves, which are attached by thin, flexible stems, shimmer in the slightest breeze. During the fall, the deciduous leaves turn brilliant shades of yellow, orange, and red, often slashing entire mountainsides with color. Aspens propagate via their root system, so that many hundreds of trees forming a stand are actually the same plant. They are often the first tree to grow back after a forest fire because young aspens can tolerate open sunlight better than most evergreen seedlings. Quaking aspen only lives about one hundred years, but the aspen groves provide shade for the longer-lived firs and spruces to get a start. By the time the aspens are reaching old age, the evergreen trees are already replacing them.

In many areas, aspen groves harbor arborglyphs, or historic tree carvings. Mostly done by sheepherders of Basque ancestry, many of the carvings date back fifty years or more. Subjects range from simple lists of names to detailed depictions of people, wildlife, and buildings.

Aspen bark is soft and easy to carve, but don't be tempted yourself. Old aspen carvings are historic artifacts protected by law, but there are far too many of us now to indulge in tree carving.

Miles and Directions

0.0 Leave the Trail Canyon Trailhead on the Trail Canyon Trail.

1.8 Arrive at Cockscomb Ridge saddle and viewpoint, the destination for the hike; return the way you came.

3.6 Arrive back at Trail Canyon Trailhead.

6 Cathedral Rock

This hike climbs through the vertical limestone cliffs on the south side of Kyle Canyon to Cathedral Rock. From this rocky summit, you can see Mount Charleston and Mary Jane Falls.

Distance: 2.6 miles out and back

Approximate hiking time: 2 hours

Difficulty: Moderate due to elevation gain

Trail surface: Dirt and rocks

Best season: Spring through fall

Water availability: None

Other trail users: Equestrians

Canine compatibility: Dogs allowed on leashes

Fees and permits: None

Maps: USGS: Charleston Peak

Trail contacts: Spring Mountains National Recreation Area, Humboldt-Toiyabe National Forest, 4701 N. Torrey Pines Dr., Las Vegas 89130-2301; (702) 515-5400; www.fs.fed.us/r4/htnf/districts/smnra

Special considerations: Although the air is cool at these high elevations, it is dry and you may not realize how much moisture you are losing. Carry and drink plenty of water, and use a good sunscreen.

Finding the trailhead: From Las Vegas, drive approximately 15 miles northwest on US 95, and then turn left onto NV 157 (Kyle Canyon Road). Continue 20.7 miles and follow NV 157 as it turns sharply left. Park at Cathedral Rock Picnic Area and Trailhead. GPS: UTM 11S 621767E 4013193N

The Hike

The South Loop Trail also leaves this trailhead; stay right on the Cathedral Rock Trail. A series of broad switchbacks climb a ravine between the towering cliffs. This ravine is an active avalanche path in winter, as evidenced by the lack of tall trees. Only low brush and limber aspen trees manage to survive the repeated slides. Watch for a seasonal waterfall off the trail to the left, which is accessible via short spur trail. Flow at the waterfall is greatest in the spring. When the trail reaches the saddle below Cathedral Rock, bear right to reach the summit. This 8,500-foot summit offers sweeping views of spectacular Kyle Canyon, including Mary Jane Falls to the northwest near the head of the canyon. You can also see the 11,811-foot summit of Charleston Peak to the west, and the pinnacles of Cockscomb Ridge to the north.

Snow avalanches are common in the higher mountain ranges of Nevada. Avalanche paths are mostly found on north- and east-facing slopes, where the prevailing storm winds cause snow to accumulate, and the low winter sun fails to melt it. Uniform stands of small trees often mark avalanche paths, all the trees having started growing at the same time after a major avalanche. The dry, light snow that falls in the intermountain West, and the cold, clear weather between storms, favor the development of an unstable snowpack. If a shallow layer of snow lies on the mountainsides for an extended period, which is common after a series of fall storms followed by clear weather, snow physics causes very weak snow crystals to develop. Later in the winter, when more snow falls on this weak layer, it may fail, causing a large avalanche that takes off all the snow cover and destroys trees that are hundreds of years old.

Although it is clear that snow avalanches are a major natural force in the Spring Mountains, it is less clear whether glaciers have ever had a hand in carving these mountains. At first glance, the steep, cliff-bound canyons, such as Kyle and Lee Canyons, appear somewhat glacial in form. But no

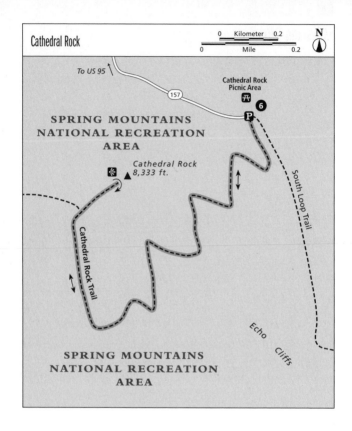

Cathedral Rock

SPRING MOUNTAINS
NATIONAL RECREATION
AREA

Cathedral Rock
8,333 ft.

Cathedral Rock Trail

South Loop Trail

To US 95

Cathedral Rock
Picnic Area

6

Echo Cliffs

SPRING MOUNTAINS
NATIONAL RECREATION
AREA

definitive evidence of past glaciers has been found in the Spring Mountains. Such features as glacial till—unsorted deposits of rocks, sand, and gravel—and moraines—the piles of rock bulldozed up by moving ice—are found in Nevada ranges lying farther north, but not in the Spring Mountains.

Miles and Directions

0.0 Leave Cathedral Rock Trailhead on the Cathedral Rock Trail.

1.2 The Cathedral Rock Trail crosses a saddle; bear right to walk to the summit of Cathedral Rock.

1.3 Arrive at Cathedral Rock, the destination for the hike; now, return the way you came.

2.6 Arrive back at Cathedral Rock Trailhead.

7 South Loop Trail

This hike uses a portion of the South Loop Trail to reach a 9,000-foot overlook above Kyle Canyon. The viewpoint offers views of rugged Kyle Canyon and the summits along the ridge east of Charleston Peak.

Distance: 3.6 miles out and back
Approximate hiking time: 5 hours
Difficulty: Moderate due to elevation gain
Trail surface: Dirt and rocks
Best season: Spring through fall
Water availability: None
Other trail users: Equestrians
Canine compatibility: Dogs allowed on leashes
Fees and permits: None
Maps: USGS: Charleston Peak

Trail contacts: Spring Mountains National Recreation Area, Humboldt-Toiyabe National Forest, 4701 N. Torrey Pines Dr., Las Vegas 89130-2301; (702) 515-5400; www.fs.fed.us/r4/htnf/districts/smnra
Special considerations: Although the air is cool at these high elevations, it is dry and you may not realize how much moisture you are losing. Carry and drink plenty of water, and use a good sunscreen.

Finding the trailhead: From Las Vegas, drive approximately 15 miles northwest on US 95, and then turn left onto NV 157 (Kyle Canyon Road). Continue 20.7 miles and follow NV 157 as it turns sharply left. Park at Cathedral Rock Picnic Area and Trailhead. GPS: UTM 11S 621767E 4013193N

The Hike

Cathedral Rock Trail also starts from this trailhead; bear left on the South Loop Trail. Initially, the South Loop Trail climbs gradually south, skirting below the massive limestone Echo Cliffs. It crosses a ravine and turns southeast, continuing to climb across the slopes below the cliffs. After crossing a second ravine, the South Loop Trail turns to the south and climbs into a break in the cliffs at the head of the second ravine. Steep, short switchbacks now lead west up a steep slope, and then the South Loop Trail climbs north to a viewpoint at the top of the Echo Cliffs. This stunning viewpoint, with a fine view of Kyle Canyon and the Spring Mountains, is the turnaround point for the hike. To the west, you have a view of the steep north ridges dropping from the summit ridge of Charleston Peak, and to the south, you're looking at 11,053-foot Griffith Peak.

The South Loop Trail continues to the summit of Charleston Peak, where it joins the North Loop Trail. For details on this difficult and strenuous hike, see my Falcon-Guide *Hiking Nevada*.

While enjoying the view, you might be visited by a rare rodent, the Palmer chipmunk, which is a protected species found only in the Spring Mountains. It can be identified by its reddish-brown fur, changing to gray at the shoulders, with black stripes down the back. They are omnivorous and live on the ground, usually in burrows. Some burrows can reach 30 feet in length. The main threats to the Palmer chipmunk's survival are development on the mountain and impacts from visitors. You can help by not feeding the chipmunks (or any other wildlife). Human food makes the chipmunks dependent on handouts, so that they lose their foraging skills and starve to death during the winter.

Two of the common high-elevation trees in the Spring Mountains are limber and whitebark pines. Both trees have needles that grow in bunches of five. Both trees have very flexible branches that readily give to shed snow loads, in

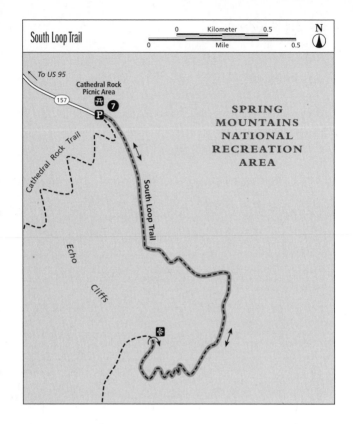

South Loop Trail

SPRING MOUNTAINS NATIONAL RECREATION AREA

To US 95

Cathedral Rock Picnic Area

157

Cathedral Rock Trail

South Loop Trail

Echo Cliffs

contrast to the spruces, which have stiff, downward-slanting branches in order to shed snow. The cones are the key to distinguishing these otherwise very similar trees. Limber pine cones are green with a turpentine odor and open to release the seeds; whitebark cones are purple with a sweet odor, and remain closed. Whitebark pines are dependent on the Clark's nutcracker, a timberline bird that removes the seeds from the cones and caches them. Seeds that are not retrieved often germinate.

Miles and Directions

0.0   Leave Cathedral Rock Trailhead on the South Loop Trail.

0.5   The South Loop Trail crosses the first ravine.

1.3   The start of a series of switchbacks on the South Loop Trail.

1.8   Arrive at the viewpoint, the destination for the hike; return the way you came.

3.6   Arrive back at Cathedral Rock Trailhead.

8 Mummy Spring

This hike features a spring and one of the largest bristlecone pines in the Spring Mountains. Bristlecone pines reach ages of more than 4,700 years, and their gaunt, twisted forms are mute testimony to the difficulties of life near the timberline.

Distance: 5.2 miles out and back
Approximate hiking time: 4 hours
Difficulty: Moderate due to elevation gain
Trail surface: Dirt and rocks
Best season: Spring through fall
Water availability: Mummy Spring
Other trail users: Equestrians
Canine compatibility: Dogs allowed on leashes
Fees and permits: None
Maps: USGS: Charleston Peak

Trail contacts: Spring Mountains National Recreation Area, Humboldt-Toiyabe National Forest, 4701 N. Torrey Pines Dr., Las Vegas 89130-2301; (702) 515-5400; www.fs.fed.us/r4/htnf/districts/smnra
Special considerations: Although the air is cool at these high elevations, it is dry and you may not realize how much moisture you are losing. Carry and drink plenty of water, and use a good sunscreen.

Finding the trailhead: From Las Vegas, drive approximately 15 miles northwest on US 95, and then turn left onto NV 157 (Kyle Canyon Road). Continue 17.6 miles, and then turn right onto NV 158. Drive 5.0 miles, and park at the trailhead on the left. This trailhead is just past Hilltop Campground. GPS: UTM 11S 624521E 4019115N

The Hike

From the trailhead, follow the North Loop Trail southwest up a ravine through stands of ponderosa pine and white fir.

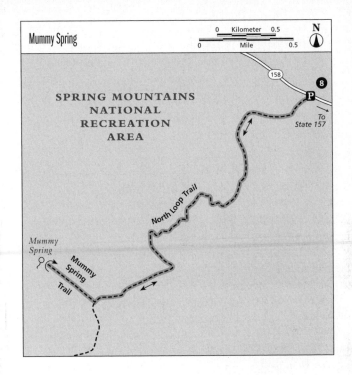

Coming out onto a broad slope, the trail works its way west and south, climbing steadily. Finally, the North Loop Trail levels out along the crest of the main ridge. At the point where the North Loop Trail leaves the crest and contours south along a slope, turn right onto the Mummy Spring Trail.

At the trail junction is one of the largest bristlecone pines in the Spring Mountains. These gnarled, slow-growing trees live for more than 4,700 years—much of the span of recorded human history. The wood is dense and resinous and resists attack by insects and disease. Bristlecone pines get their name from the short bristles on their pinecones. The cones, and the short, stiff needles, which grow in tight bunches of five, make it easy to identify the tree. The oldest trees live near timberline, where the growing conditions are harsh: short summers and extreme winter weather. Often a bristlecone will appear to be mostly dead, but a strip of living bark still provides nutrients to a single live branch. Even after they die, the wood is resistant to decay and insects because of its large sap content. Dead bristlecone wood can lie on the high mountainsides for thousands of years and can be tree ring dated just like the live trees, extending our knowledge of climate further into the past. The valuable record provided by both living and dead wood is one of several reasons why wood should not be burned in campfires near timberline.

Now, follow the Mummy Spring Trail as it descends slightly through more bristlecone pines. The trail ends at Mummy Spring, a mecca for wildlife and the turnaround point for the hike.

Miles and Directions

0.0 Leave the North Loop Trailhead on the North Loop Trail.

1.8 The North Loop Trail levels out along the ridge crest.

2.3 Turn right onto Mummy Spring Trail.

2.6 Arrive at Mummy Spring, the destination for the hike; return the way you came.

5.2 Arrive back at North Loop Trailhead.

⑨ Bristlecone Trail

This loop trail passes through an extensive stand of ancient bristlecone pines. This is one of the few Spring Mountains trails open to mountain bikers.

Distance: 5.4-mile loop
Approximate hiking time: 3 hours
Difficulty: Moderate due to elevation gain
Trail surface: Dirt and rocks
Best season: Spring through fall
Water availability: None
Other trail users: Equestrians and mountain bikers
Canine compatibility: Dogs allowed on leashes
Fees and permits: None
Maps: USGS: Charleston Peak

Trail contacts: Spring Mountains National Recreation Area, Humboldt-Toiyabe National Forest, 4701 N. Torrey Pines Dr., Las Vegas 89130-2301; (702) 515-5400; www.fs.fed.us/r4/htnf/districts/smnra

Special considerations: Although the air is cool at these high elevations, it is dry and you may not realize how much moisture you are losing. Carry and drink plenty of water, and use a good sunscreen.

Finding the trailhead: From Las Vegas, drive approximately 29 miles northwest on US 95, and then turn left onto NV 156. Continue 17.4 miles to the Upper Bristlecone Trailhead at the end of the road at the upper parking lot of the Lee Canyon Ski Area. GPS: UTM 11S 618657E 4018871N

The Hike

At first, the trail heads southwest up a canyon bottom filled with an alpine forest of fir and aspen. After the Bristlecone Trail makes a sharp right turn and climbs out of the canyon to the north, it crosses a more exposed slope where living conditions are much tougher than the canyon bottom you

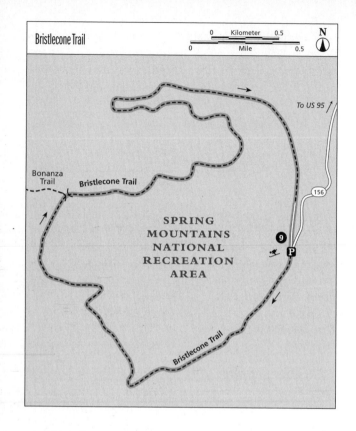

just left. These are exactly the conditions that bristlecone pines favor. In fact, the Spring Mountains have extensive stands of bristlecones: some 18,000 acres.

Bristlecone pines actually do grow well below timberline, where they are taller and more slender than their gnarled timberline counterparts. But the easy living exacts a price: "Low elevation" bristlecone pines rarely live to 1,000 years before succumbing to disease, rot, or insects.

The trail descends slightly to a saddle and meets the Bonanza Trail; stay right on the Bristlecone Trail. This section of trail is wider; it follows a now-abandoned road built by the Works Project Administration during the 1930s. The WPA and its sister "alphabet agencies" provided employment for thousands of people during the Great Depression and constructed roads, trails, bridges, and campgrounds throughout the national forests.

Continue on the Bristlecone Trail as it heads east along the south slopes of a ridge. The trail swings around the east end of this ridge and descends into Scout Canyon in one long switchback to the west. The trail then turns east, and then south, to end at the Lower Bristlecone Trailhead. Walk a short distance down the dirt road to NV 156, then follow the highway south to the upper parking lot at Lee Canyon Ski Area and your vehicle at Upper Bristlecone Trailhead.

Miles and Directions

0.0 Leave Upper Bristlecone Trailhead on the Bristlecone Trail.

1.0 The Bristlecone Trail turns abruptly right (north) and leaves the canyon.

1.7 Cross the high point of the loop.

2.2 Reach the junction with the Bonanza Trail in a saddle; stay right to remain on the Bristlecone Trail.

4.9 Arrive at Lower Bristlecone Trailhead; now, follow the dirt road a few yards to NV 156, then follow the highway south to the Upper Bristlecone Trailhead.

5.4 Arrive back at Upper Bristlecone Trailhead.

Red Rock Canyon National Conservation Area

The Red Rock Canyon National Conservation Area was established to protect the unique area of towering red sandstone cliffs and canyons west of Las Vegas. A 13-mile scenic drive, several picnic areas, a campground, and a visitor center attract more than a million visitors a year. The Red Rocks, as they are called by the locals, are a rock climber's mecca, and hundreds of routes have been established on the walls. The Red Rocks also have the largest concentration of trails in the Las Vegas area, making it special for hikers as well.

Because of the relatively low elevation, spring and fall are the best times to visit the Red Rocks. Summers are very hot, while during the winter, snow may linger in some of the shady canyons. Still, during the clear periods between storms, the Red Rocks can be explored in the winter. During late summer, afternoon thunderstorms are common, so hikers should avoid narrow, flood-prone canyons when heavy rain is a possibility.

The stunning geology of the Red Rocks is due to the fact that massive, red cliffs of Aztec sandstone are overlain by older, gray limestone in a reversal of the normal order, in which younger rocks are deposited on top of older rocks. At the Red Rocks, the Keystone Thrust Fault pushed the older rocks over the top of the younger rocks, a common occurrence during mountain-building.

Backcountry camping is allowed above 5,000 feet, but there are few permanent water sources, and campfires are prohibited at all times. There are no developed trails in the backcountry.

Mountain biking is not allowed on any of the trails in this section but is allowed on a trail system in the Cottonwood Valley, about 10 miles south of the visitor center off NV 160.

10 Moenkopi Trail

This is an easy day hike on an interpretive nature trail.

Distance: 2.2-mile loop
Approximate hiking time: 1 hour
Difficulty: Easy
Trail surface: Dirt and rocks
Best season: Fall through spring
Water availability: None
Other trail users: None
Canine compatibility: Dogs allowed on leashes
Fees and permits: Entrance fee
Maps: USGS: La Madre Mountain

Trail contacts: Bureau of Land Management, Southern Nevada District Office, 4701 N. Torrey Pines Dr., Las Vegas 89130; (702) 515-5000; www.blm.gov/ nv/st/en/fo/lvfo/blm_programs/ blm_special_areas/red_rock_ nca.html
Special considerations: During the summer, hike early in the day and carry plenty of water.

Finding the trailhead: From Las Vegas, drive west on Charleston Boulevard (NV 159) to reach the start of the Red Rock Scenic Loop, which is 10.7 miles from the intersection of Charleston and Rainbow Boulevards. Turn right (north) onto the Scenic Loop road, then immediately left to the Bureau of Land Management Visitor Center. Here you can obtain general information on the Red Rock area and check on the road and trail conditions. GPS: UTM 11S 641519E 3999922N

The Hike

The Moenkopi Trail starts southwest of the visitor center near the weather station. Along the way, watch for creosote, blackbrush, and yucca, typical members of this desert plant community. The trail leads to the crest of the hill west of the visitor center. At the crest, cottontop barrel cactus and Triassic fossils can be seen.

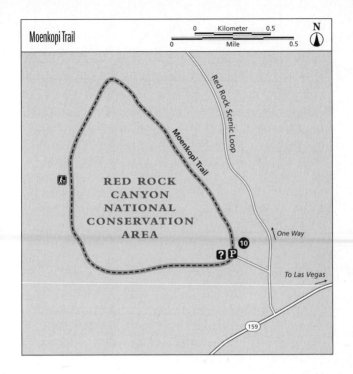

Creosote bush, found along this trail and common in southern Nevada and the rest of the Mohave Desert, is an outstanding example of the extreme methods desert plants use to survive drought. During dry periods, the bush sheds its mature leaves as well as whole twigs and branches, retaining only the new leaves. These leaves can lose well over half their water and still survive. In comparison, humans are seriously ill after a water loss of only five percent.

Barrel cactus uses another strategy to survive in the desert. Rather than economizing on water during dry periods as the creosote bush does, the barrel cactus uses a widespread but shallow root system to rapidly collect groundwater after a rain. It then stores the moisture in the fleshy interior of the plant. Protecting this succulent interior is a nest of curved, overlapping, and very sharp spines. Desert lore has it that a thirsty traveler can break open a barrel cactus and dip out a cool drink. In reality, all you'll find is a bitter green core after getting past the cactus's formidable defenses.

Because this loop is a simple nature trail, specific miles and directions are not included here.

11 Calico Tanks

An easy day hike to natural water tanks in the red rock Calico Hills. Such water tanks are vital for wildlife, and they were important for natives and settlers.

Distance: 2.0 miles out and back
Approximate hiking time: 1 hour
Difficulty: Easy
Trail surface: Dirt and rocks
Best season: Fall through spring
Water availability: None
Other trail users: None
Canine compatibility: Dogs allowed on leashes
Fees and permits: Entrance fee
Maps: USGS: La Madre Mountain

Trail contacts: Bureau of Land Management, Southern Nevada District Office, 4701 N. Torrey Pines Dr., Las Vegas 89130; (702) 515-5000; www.blm.gov/nv/st/en/fo/lvfo/blm_programs/blm_special_areas/red_rock_nca.html
Special considerations: During the summer, hike early in the day and carry plenty of water.

Finding the trailhead: From Las Vegas, drive west on Charleston Boulevard (NV 159) to reach the start of the Red Rock Scenic Loop, which is 10.7 miles from the intersection of Charleston and Rainbow Boulevards. Turn right (north) onto the Scenic Loop road (one-way), and drive 2.7 miles to Sandstone Quarry, on the right, and park. GPS: UTM 11S 639409E 4003207N

The Hike

Follow the wash north 0.25 mile, then turn right (east) at the third canyon and continue up a side canyon through the red slickrock to a large natural water tank (tinaja). When they have water, this and other tinajas in the Calico Hills are important sources of water for the area's wildlife.

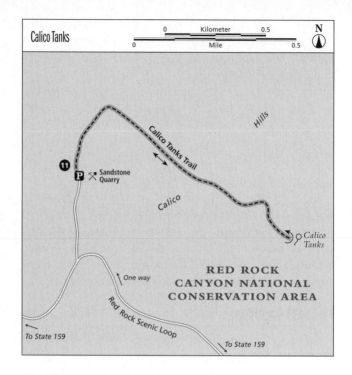

Tinaja is Spanish for "tank." Most natural desert water tanks are smaller than this one and tend to form where cascading flood waters have scoured out deep basins in the bedrock underlying normally dry washes. They tend to occur in deep canyons where the additional shade helps keep the water from evaporating. In many desert ranges, tinajas are the only year-round source of water for wildlife. Hikers can use the water as well but should observe a few commonsense courtesies. Take only the water you need, and use it sparingly for all purposes except drinking. Never bathe in a tinaja or pollute it with soap or food scraps. Others will need the water. Avoid camping nearby, as your presence will scare away the animals that normally come to drink during the night. Finally, water from a tinaja should always be purified before drinking or cooking with it.

The origin and exact meaning of the term "slickrock" is unclear. It is generally used in the American Southwest to describe areas of exposed sandstone such as the Calico Hills. In arid climates sandstone often erodes to form sleekly rounded domes and turrets. From a distance the term "slickrock" is descriptive, but up close, the hiker will discover that the rock is anything but slick. It is nature's sandpaper, composed of billions of grains of sand cemented together by heat and pressure. Contrary to popular opinion, slickrock country is primarily eroded by water during occasional desert storms. Wind plays a very minor role.

Miles and Directions

0.0 Leave the Sandstone Quarry Trailhead and follow the Calico Tanks Trail up the wash.

1.0 Arrive at Calico Tanks; now, return the way you came.

2.0 Arrive back at Sandstone Quarry Trailhead.

12 Keystone Thrust

An easy day hike to an overlook above the Keystone Thrust Fault contact zone, a place where older rocks have been overturned and thrust on top of younger rocks.

Distance: 2.0 miles out and back
Approximate hiking time: 1 hour
Difficulty: Easy
Trail surface: Dirt and rocks
Best season: Fall through spring
Water availability: None
Other trail users: None
Canine compatibility: Dogs allowed on leashes
Fees and permits: Entrance fee
Maps: USGS: La Madre Mountain

Trail contacts: Bureau of Land Management, Southern Nevada District Office, 4701 N. Torrey Pines Dr., Las Vegas 89130; (702) 515-5000; www.blm.gov/nv/st/en/fo/lvfo/blm_programs/blm_special_areas/red_rock_nca.html
Special considerations: During the summer, hike early in the day and carry plenty of water.

Finding the trailhead: From Las Vegas, drive west on Charleston Boulevard (NV 159) to reach the start of the Red Rock Scenic Loop, which is 10.7 miles from the intersection of Charleston and Rainbow Boulevards. Turn right (north) onto the Scenic Loop road (one-way), then drive 5.9 miles to White Rock Spring parking area and turn right. Follow the dirt road 0.9 mile to the White Rock Spring Trailhead, at road's end, and park. GPS: UTM 11S 636964E 4004042N

The Hike

Walk 100 yards back down the road (east) to a closed dirt road now on your left (north). Follow the old road across the wash, where it turns left and starts to climb the ridge opposite the trailhead. After approximately 0.75 mile the trail crosses a wash and climbs into a small saddle. Just up

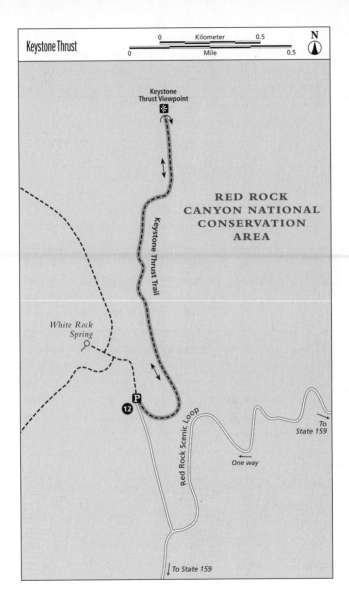

Keystone Thrust

0 Kilometer 0.5
0 Mile 0.5

N

Keystone
Thrust Viewpoint

RED ROCK
CANYON NATIONAL
CONSERVATION
AREA

Keystone Thrust Trail

White Rock
Spring

P

12

Red Rock Scenic Loop

One way

To
State 159

To State 159

the ridge, the trail forks, with the right fork descending off the ridge into a small canyon. The contact of the Keystone Thrust Fault is visible below, where the older gray limestone has been forced over the top of the much younger red and white Aztec sandstone.

A thrust fault is a fracture in the earth's crust where one rock layer is thrust horizontally over another. Normally younger rocks are found on top of older rocks, as they are deposited in layered succession. But here the older limestone has been pushed over the top of the younger sandstone. It is believed that this occurred about sixty-five million years ago when two continental plates collided to create the current North American continent. The thrust contact is clearly defined by the sharp contrast between the gray limestones and the red sandstones. The Keystone Thrust Fault extends from the Cottonwood Fault (along the Pahrump Highway) 13 miles northward to the vicinity of La Madre Mountain, where it is obscured by more complex faulting. Thrust faults are common in mountainous regions because of the violence of the forces that created the mountains, but the Keystone Thrust Fault is one of the best exposed in the world.

In regions such as the Alps, multiple thrust faults created very complex layering in the rock. Later erosion removed much of the original rock, making the thrust faults much less obvious and confusing the relationships between rocks. Early geologists found such thrust fault regions difficult to decipher.

Miles and Directions

0.0 Leave the White Rock Spring Trailhead and walk back down the dirt road, then turn left onto an old, closed dirt road.

1.0 Arrive at Keystone Thrust Viewpoint; return the way you came.

2.0 Arrive back at White Rock Spring Trailhead.

13 White Rock Hills

An easy day hike on an informal trail to a vantage point that features a dramatic view of the valley containing La Madre Spring.

Distance: 2.6 miles out and back

Approximate hiking time: 2 hours

Difficulty: Easy

Trail surface: Dirt and rocks

Best season: Fall through spring

Water availability: None

Other trail users: None

Canine compatibility: Dogs allowed on leashes

Fees and permits: Entrance fee

Maps: USGS: La Madre Mountain

Trail contacts: Bureau of Land Management, Southern Nevada District Office, 4701 N. Torrey Pines Dr., Las Vegas 89130; (702) 515-5000; www.blm.gov/ nv/st/en/fo/lvfo/blm_programs/ blm_special_areas/red_rock_ nca.html

Special considerations: During the summer, hike early in the day and carry plenty of water.

Finding the trailhead: From Las Vegas, drive west on Charleston Boulevard (NV 159) to reach the start of the Red Rock Scenic Loop, which is 10.7 miles from the intersection of Charleston and Rainbow Boulevards. Turn right (north) onto the Scenic Loop road (one-way), then drive 5.9 miles to White Rock Spring parking area and turn right. Follow the dirt road 0.9 mile to the White Rock Spring Trailhead, at road's end, and park. GPS: UTM 11S 636964E 4004042N

The Hike

Go west down a short closed road, which drops into the wash to the right of the White Rock Hills. Then continue up the wash along the base of the sandstone bluffs. After about 0.5 mile an informal trail veers out of the wash to the

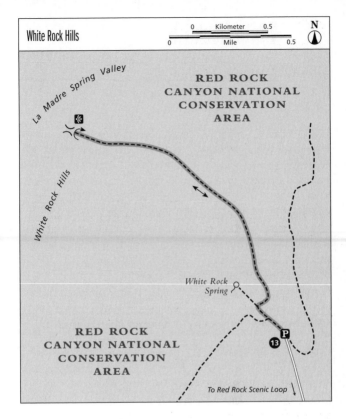

right. A few cairns mark the route as it parallels the wash. About 2 miles from the trailhead, the route reaches a saddle with excellent views of the west side of the White Rock Hills and the valley above La Madre Spring. The towering limestone cliffs of La Madre Mountain to the north make a somber contrast with the bright sandstone to the left.

Once again, the Keystone Thrust Fault is responsible for the fact that the younger sandstones of the White Rock Hills are found below the older limestone layers. The younger, brighter layers of Aztec sandstone even *look* younger than the gray limestones.

Miles and Directions

0.0 Leave the White Rock Spring Trailhead, and go west down an old dirt road.

0.5 Follow the trail as it veers out of the wash to the right.

1.3 Reach the saddle overlooking La Madre Spring Valley; return the way you came.

2.6 Arrive back at White Rock Spring Trailhead.

14 White Rock Spring to Willow Spring

This trail connects White Rock Spring and Willow Spring, running along the steep base of the White Rock Hills.

Distance: 3.0 miles out and back
Approximate hiking time: 2 hours
Difficulty: Easy
Trail surface: Dirt and rocks
Best season: Fall through spring
Water availability: None
Other trail users: None
Canine compatibility: Dogs allowed on leashes
Fees and permits: Entrance fee

Maps: USGS: La Madre Mountain
Trail contacts: Bureau of Land Management, Southern Nevada District Office, 4701 N. Torrey Pines Dr., Las Vegas 89130; (702) 515-5000; www.blm.gov/nv/st/en/fo/lvfo/blm_programs/blm_special_areas/red_rock_nca.html
Special considerations: During the summer, hike early in the day and carry plenty of water.

Finding the trailhead: From Las Vegas, drive west on Charleston Boulevard (NV 159) to reach the start of the Red Rock Scenic Loop, which is 10.7 miles from the intersection of Charleston and Rainbow Boulevards. Turn right (north) onto the Scenic Loop road (one-way), then drive 5.9 miles to the White Rock Spring parking area and turn right. Follow the dirt road 0.9 mile to the White Rock Spring Trailhead, at road's end, and park. GPS: UTM 11S 636964E 4004042N

The Hike

The trail is the closed dirt road on the left (west). Follow the closed dirt road toward the water catchment. Just before reaching the catchment, the trail to Willow Spring can be located on the left, heading in a southwesterly direction. The trail follows along the base of the White Rock Hills and

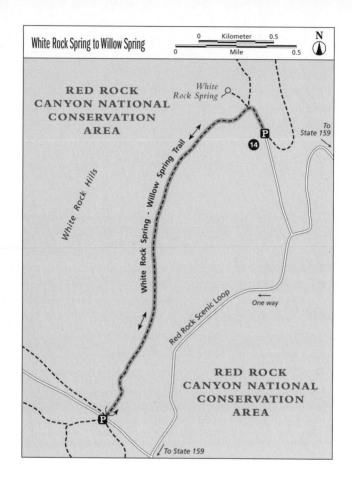

RED ROCK
CANYON NATIONAL
CONSERVATION
AREA

White Rock Hills

White Rock Spring - Willow Spring Trail

White
Rock Spring

To State 159

Red Rock Scenic Loop

One way

RED ROCK
CANYON NATIONAL
CONSERVATION
AREA

To State 159

joins the Willow Spring Trail across from the Lost Creek parking area.

Along this trail, or almost anywhere in the Nevada desert, you are likely to see one of the American desert's most common mammals: the jackrabbit with its large, black-tipped ears. This large rabbit is commonly seen bounding across roads and can be numerous in good years. The large ears contain many blood vessels and serve to radiate heat to the environment, as well as alerting the jackrabbit to the presence of predators. The jackrabbit's predators include hawks, foxes, and coyotes.

Since man has exterminated the wolf throughout most of its former range, coyotes have filled in the predatory niche once occupied by wolves and have spread throughout much of the country. Coyotes are smart and versatile hunters and will eat carrion as well as live prey. Mice, other small rodents, and rabbits are the coyote's main prey.

Miles and Directions

0.0 Leave the White Rock Spring Trailhead, and walk down the closed road to the west. Before reaching the water catchment, turn left onto the trail to Willow Spring.

1.5 Arrive at Lost Creek Trailhead; return the way you came.

3.0 Arrive back at White Rock Spring Trailhead.

15 Lost Creek Loop

This loop hike to a box canyon features a seasonal waterfall. The waterfall is best in the spring after a snowy winter provides plenty of snowmelt.

Distance: 0.7-mile loop
Approximate hiking time: 1 hour
Difficulty: Easy
Trail surface: Dirt and rocks
Best season: Fall through spring
Water availability: None
Other trail users: None
Canine compatibility: Dogs allowed on leashes
Fees and permits: Entrance fee
Maps: USGS: La Madre Mountain

Trail contacts: Bureau of Land Management, Southern Nevada District Office, 4701 N. Torrey Pines Dr., Las Vegas 89130; (702) 515-5000; www.blm.gov/ nv/st/en/fo/lvfo/blm_programs/ blm_special_areas/red_rock_ nca.html

Special considerations: During the summer, hike early in the day and carry plenty of water.

Finding the trailhead: From Las Vegas, drive west on Charleston Boulevard (NV 159) to reach the start of the Red Rock Scenic Loop, which is 10.7 miles from the intersection of Charleston and Rainbow Boulevards. Turn right (north) onto the Scenic Loop road (one-way), then drive 7.0 miles to the Lost Creek Trailhead, on the right, and park. GPS: UTM 11S 635994E 4002242N

The Hike

Take either the right or left loop to the creek, with its permanent water. You can continue upstream to a box canyon with a seasonal waterfall.

A box canyon is a canyon with no outlet at its upper end. Sometimes the obstacle is a jumble of boulders block-

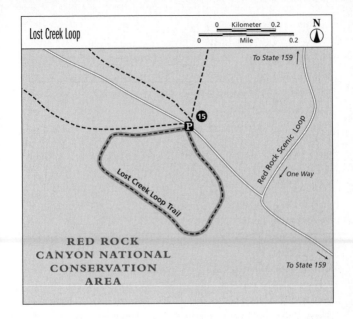

0   Kilometer   0.2

0   Mile   0.2

N

To State 159

Red Rock Scenic Loop

15

P

One Way

Lost Creek Loop Trail

RED ROCK
CANYON NATIONAL
CONSERVATION
AREA

To State 159

ing the canyon floor or, as is the case here, a seasonal waterfall. Smaller canyons are more likely than larger ones to "box up." The reason is that canyons erode headward, toward the steeper slopes. Rain falling on steep slopes runs downhill at a much higher speed than water running down gentler gradients. The ability of water to transport silt, sand, pebbles, and rocks increases rapidly as the speed of flow increases, so erosion proceeds much faster at the heads of canyons than it does lower down. As the canyon head erodes, it undermines the slopes above, causing them to collapse, much like a child digging into a sandpile until it collapses. If the headward erosion of the canyon encounters a harder layer of rock, a drop-off or pour-off often forms, resulting in a box canyon.

Storm water pouring off a seasonal waterfall often erodes out a "plunge pool" out of the bedrock at the base of the fall. Some plunge pools may be quite deep, and since plunge pools tend to form at the base of falls in deep, narrow canyons, where they are shaded from the sun much of the time, some larger plunge pools contain water year-round. Where canyons emerge from the mountains, as along the Red Rock Escarpment, plunge pools tend to form where the canyons exit the mountains.

Because this very short loop is easy to follow, specific miles and directions are not included.

16 Willow Spring Loop

This hike features a variety of plant communities, including riparian streamside, pines, oaks, and sagebrush desert. You can also see prehistoric roasting pits, used by natives to roast food.

Distance: 1.5-mile loop
Approximate hiking time: 1 hour
Difficulty: Easy
Trail surface: Dirt and rocks
Best season: Fall through spring
Water availability: None
Other trail users: None
Canine compatibility: Dogs allowed on leashes
Fees and permits: Entrance fee
Maps: USGS: La Madre Mountain

Trail contacts: Bureau of Land Management, Southern Nevada District Office, 4701 N. Torrey Pines Dr., Las Vegas 89130; (702) 515-5000; www.blm.gov/nv/st/en/fo/lvfo/blm_programs/blm_special_areas/red_rock_nca.html
Special considerations: During the summer, hike early in the day and carry plenty of water.

Finding the trailhead: From Las Vegas, drive west on Charleston Boulevard (NV 159) to reach the start of the Red Rock Scenic Loop, which is 10.7 miles from the intersection of Charleston and Rainbow Boulevards. Turn right (north) onto the Scenic Loop road (one-way), then drive 7.0 miles to the Willow Spring Picnic Area turnoff, and turn right. Continue 0.7 mile to the Willow Spring Picnic Area and Trailhead. GPS: UTM 11S 635084E 4002819N

The Hike

The trail follows the left (northeast) side of the canyon, past Native American roasting pits, to the Lost Creek parking area. The right-hand trail then crosses Red Rock Wash,

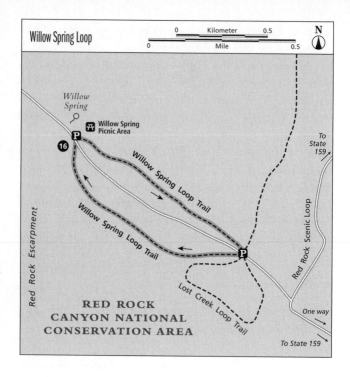

Kilometer
0   0.5
Mile
0   0.5

N

Willow Spring

Willow Spring
Picnic Area

16

Willow Spring Loop Trail

Willow Spring Loop Trail

Red Rock Escarpment

Lost Creek Loop Trail

Red Rock Scenic Loop

To State 159

One way

To State 159

**RED ROCK
CANYON NATIONAL
CONSERVATION AREA**

branches to the right, and parallels the Red Rock Escarpment and returns to Willow Spring.

Roasting pits were used by the ancient inhabitants for slow-cooking. Agave plants, other vegetables, and meats were placed in a bed of hot coals mixed with cobbles and covered with plant materials and earth. After enough time had passed, the cooked food, ash, and fire-cracked rock were dug out. The discarded rock and ash form a doughnut-shaped ring often several feet high and containing thousands of heating rocks. The vast quantity of rocks shows how long some of these pits were in use. Also known as mescal pits, these cooking sites are common in the Southwest.

Another important food source for natives and wildlife alike is the singleleaf pinyon pine. The singleleaf pinyon is easily recognized since it is the only pine with needles growing singly rather than in bunches of two or more. Like its cousin the Colorado pinyon, the seeds are edible and used to be an important food source for the native inhabitants, who would gather in temporary villages in places where the pine nut harvest was good. Pine nuts are a human delicacy often used in Southwestern-style cooking and are still an important food source for birds and small mammals.

Juniper trees commonly grow in association with pinyon pines, forming a forest community called pinyon-juniper woodland, or PJ for short. Pinyons tend to favor slightly higher and cooler slopes, while junipers favor slightly lower and warmer slopes. The bluish juniper berries are an important food for wildlife.

Miles and Directions

0.0 Leave Willow Spring Trailhead on the trail along the northeast side of the canyon.

0.8 Cross Red Rock Wash at Lost Creek Trailhead and stay on the Willow Spring Loop Trail.

1.5 Arrive back at Willow Spring Trailhead.

17 La Madre Spring

This hike is a good wildlife viewing opportunity. You may see bighorn sheep, deer, and other wildlife in the vicinity of La Madre Spring, which has been improved to provide a better source of water for wildlife.

Distance: 3.8 miles out and back
Approximate hiking time: 2 hours
Difficulty: Easy
Trail surface: Dirt and rocks
Best season: Fall through spring
Water availability: None
Other trail users: None
Canine compatibility: Dogs allowed on leashes
Fees and permits: Entrance fee
Maps: USGS: La Madre Mtn, La Madre Spring, Mountain Springs
Trail contacts: Bureau of Land Management, Southern Nevada District Office, 4701 N. Torrey Pines Dr., Las Vegas 89130; (702) 515-5000; www.blm.gov/nv/st/en/fo/lvfo/blm_programs/blm_special_areas/red_rock_nca.html
Special considerations: During the summer, hike early in the day and carry plenty of water.

Finding the trailhead: From Las Vegas, drive west on Charleston Boulevard (NV 159) to reach the start of the Red Rock Scenic Loop, which is 10.7 miles from the intersection of Charleston and Rainbow Boulevards. Turn right (north) onto the Scenic Loop road (one-way), then drive 7.0 miles to the Willow Spring Picnic Area turnoff, and turn right. Continue 0.7 mile to the Willow Spring Picnic Area and Trailhead. GPS: UTM 11S 635084E 4002819N

The Hike

Walk up the Rocky Gap Road, an unsigned jeep road that begins at the end of the pavement. Just after crossing the wash, turn right at an unsigned fork. A more interesting way

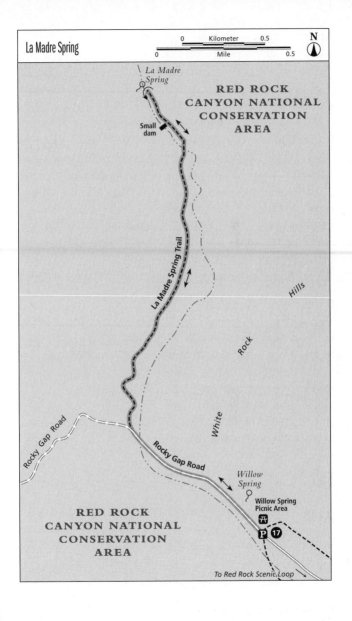

Kilometer

Mile

N

La Madre Spring

RED ROCK CANYON NATIONAL CONSERVATION AREA

Small dam

La Madre Spring Trail

Hills

Rock

White

Rocky Gap Road

Rocky Gap Road

Willow Spring

Willow Spring Picnic Area

P 17

RED ROCK CANYON NATIONAL CONSERVATION AREA

To Red Rock Scenic Loop

to reach this junction is to walk up the wash to the south of the road. After the fork, stay on the main road, which stays left (west) of the wash. Numerous unsigned roads branch off on either side. The road ends at a small dam, and a footpath leads up the creek to the spring. Bighorn sheep and other wildlife rely on the water from this spring.

This is also a good place to observe bighorn sheep, in season. You'll have the best chance of seeing bighorn sheep, as well as other wildlife, if you remain quiet while hiking. Once you are at the water catchment, find a nearby vantage point and then sit or stand quietly. Concentrate on looking above you, as bighorns prefer higher terrain where they can see predators more easily. You'll often hear bighorn sheep moving before you actually catch sight of them, since they blend into their surroundings. If you do spot a band of sheep, a good pair of binoculars will help.

Miles and Directions

- **0.0** Leave Willow Spring Trailhead and follow the Rocky Gap Road.
- **0.6** Where the Rocky Gap Road forks left, stay right on an unsigned old road.
- **1.9** Arrive at La Madre Spring; return the way you came.
- **3.8** Arrive back at Willow Spring Trailhead.

18 Top of the Escarpment

This hike leads to a 7,208-foot unnamed summit, which features excellent views of the numerous sandstone ridges and canyons that make up the Red Rock Escarpment.

Distance: 2.0 miles out and back
Approximate hiking time: 2 hours
Difficulty: Easy
Trail surface: Dirt and rocks
Best season: Fall through spring
Water availability: None
Other trail users: None
Canine compatibility: Dogs allowed on leashes
Fees and permits: Entrance fee
Maps: USGS: La Madre Mtn, La

Madre Spring, Mountain Springs
Trail contacts: Bureau of Land Management, Southern Nevada District Office, 4701 N. Torrey Pines Dr., Las Vegas 89130; (702) 515-5000; www.blm.gov/ nv/st/en/fo/lvfo/blm_programs/ blm_special_areas/red_rock_ nca.html
Special considerations: During the summer, hike early in the day and carry plenty of water.

Finding the trailhead: From Las Vegas, drive west on Charleston Boulevard (NV 159) to reach the start of the Red Rock Scenic Loop, which is 10.7 miles from the intersection of Charleston and Rainbow Boulevards. Turn right (north) onto the Scenic Loop road (one-way), then drive 7.0 miles to the Willow Spring Picnic Area turnoff, and turn right. Continue 0.7 mile to the Willow Spring Picnic Area. Drive up the Rocky Gap Road, a rough, rocky road, which requires a high-clearance, four-wheel-drive vehicle. This road begins at the end of the pavement. After 0.5 mile, stay left at a fork. Continue 3.5 miles to Red Rock Summit and park. GPS: UTM 11S 631939E 3999420N.

Alternately, Red Rock Summit may be approached from the west. From Las Vegas, drive 27 miles west on NV 160 to Mountain Springs. Continue about 3 miles, then turn right (north) onto Lovell Canyon Road. In approximately 8 miles, the road to Red Rock Sum-

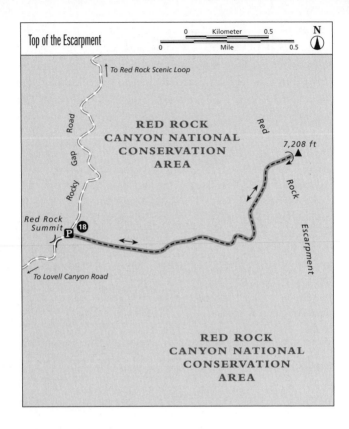

Top of the Escarpment

0   Kilometer   0.5
0   Mile   0.5

N

↑ To Red Rock Scenic Loop

Rocky Gap Road

RED ROCK
CANYON NATIONAL
CONSERVATION
AREA

Red

7,208 ft ▲

Rock

Red Rock
Summit

P 18

Escarpment

↙ To Lovell Canyon Road

RED ROCK
CANYON NATIONAL
CONSERVATION
AREA

mit turns right (east). It is about 3 miles and 1,200 feet elevation gain to the summit.

The Hike

The trail begins at Red Rock Summit and leaves the road to the east. It winds up around the head of a basin that drains to the west, and eventually reaches the crest of the escarpment. Now follow the ridge east-northeast to a spectacular viewpoint at the head of Icebox Canyon. From this 7,208-foot summit the view encompasses the Spring Mountains to the north, the entire Red Rock Canyon Area, Blue Diamond Mountain, the Las Vegas Valley, Lake Mead, the Mormon Mountains, and Mount Potosi. On clear days, you can see the 8,000-foot Virgin Mountains 85 miles away in extreme northwestern Arizona.

In the dry desert air, normal visibility is in excess of 100 miles. Spring dust storms may drop the visibility to just a few miles, as high winds pick up dust and spread it far and wide. Smog from nearby Las Vegas and even distant Los Angeles can also reduce the visibility, though not as drastically as dust storms. During the summer, smoke from forest fires can also drift over the region and reduce visibility, sometimes drastically if the fire is large or nearby.

One effect of the clear air is that it makes distant objects, such as mountain ranges or even the next ridge over, seem much closer than they are. Hikers whose experience is mostly in moister climates, where there is more haze in the air, are especially susceptible to this illusion. The solution is to depend on maps and written descriptions for distances, until you get used to the greater visibility.

As you hike back to the trailhead, look for cliffrose, a shrubby member of the rose family found growing in rocky areas at intermediate elevations in the southwestern mountains. Although cliffrose can grow to 8 feet, it is nondescript until it blooms in the spring. Then, the drab, olive green and gray plant becomes covered with hundreds of tiny, fragrant flowers. The white flowers are about 0.5 inch in size, and the leaves are tiny, only about 0.25 to 0.5 inch long. Cliffrose seeds have a long, curved hair that acts as a parachute to help disperse the seeds on the wind. Once the

19 Icebox Canyon

Featuring a seasonal waterfall and box canyon, this short hike nevertheless takes you deep into the towering cliffs of the Red Rock Escarpment.

Distance: 2.8 miles out and back
Approximate hiking time: 2 hours
Difficulty: Easy
Trail surface: Dirt and rocks
Best season: Fall through spring
Water availability: None
Other trail users: None
Canine compatibility: Dogs allowed on leashes
Fees and permits: Entrance fee
Maps: USGS: La Madre Mtn, Mountain Springs

Trail contacts: Bureau of Land Management, Southern Nevada District Office, 4701 N. Torrey Pines Dr., Las Vegas 89130; (702) 515-5000; www.blm.gov/nv/st/en/fo/lvfo/blm_programs/blm_special_areas/red_rock_nca.html
Special considerations: During the summer, hike early in the day and carry plenty of water.

Finding the trailhead: From Las Vegas, drive west on Charleston Boulevard (NV 159) to reach the start of the Red Rock Scenic Loop, which is 10.7 miles from the intersection of Charleston and Rainbow Boulevards. Turn right (north) onto the Scenic Loop road (one-way), then drive 7.4 miles to the Ice Box Canyon Overlook/Trailhead, which is on the right. GPS: UTM 11S 636504E 4001545N

The Hike

Follow the trail across the wash. The trail stays on the bench on the right (north) side of the canyon until the canyon narrows, and then ends as it drops into the wash. Follow the wash (boulder hopping is required) to a seasonal waterfall

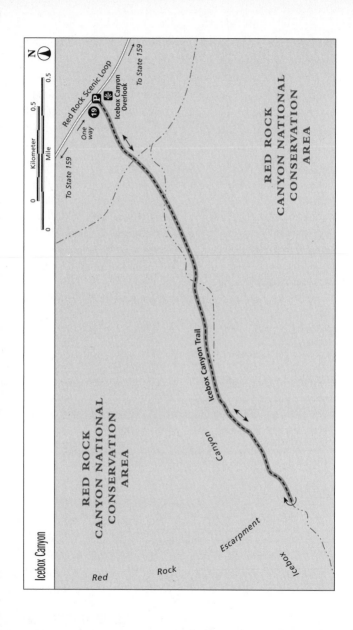

and box canyon. Icebox Canyon derives its name from the cooler temperatures in this narrow canyon.

These cooler temperatures create what are called micro-climates, small areas where the year-round climate is different enough from the surrounding area to support a plant and animal community normally found at higher elevations. An example is the presence of the huge ponderosa pines along the canyon, trees that are heat and drought resistant but do require a certain amount of water to survive. The shady depths of Icebox Canyon retard evaporation and provide a moister climate than the surrounding open desert.

Seasonal waterfalls are found all over Nevada in the numerous canyons that cut into the flanks of the mountains. At higher elevations the falls run during the snowmelt in late spring and early summer, and sometimes briefly after heavy thunderstorms. At lower elevations such as these, the falls tend to be at their best during runoff from wet, winter storms, which occur from December through March.

Miles and Directions

0.0 Leave the Icebox Canyon Trailhead on the Icebox Canyon Trail.

0.2 The trail ends; now follow the wash upstream.

1.4 Arrive at the seasonal waterfall; return the way you came.

2.8 Arrive back at the Icebox Canyon Trailhead.

20 Pine Creek Canyon

Extensive stands of ponderosa pine give this canyon its name. The trail also leads past a pioneer homestead site.

Distance: 5.0 miles out and back
Approximate hiking time: 3 hours
Difficulty: Moderate due to distance
Trail surface: Dirt and rocks
Best season: Fall through spring
Water availability: None
Other trail users: None
Canine compatibility: Dogs allowed on leashes
Fees and permits: Entrance fee

Maps: USGS: Blue Diamond, La Madre Mtn, Mountain Springs
Trail contacts: Bureau of Land Management, Southern Nevada District Office, 4701 N. Torrey Pines Dr., Las Vegas 89130; (702) 515-5000; www.blm.gov/nv/st/en/fo/lvfo/blm_programs/blm_special_areas/red_rock_nca.html
Special considerations: During the summer, hike early in the day and carry plenty of water.

Finding the trailhead: From Las Vegas, drive west on Charleston Boulevard (NV 159) to reach the start of the Red Rock Scenic Loop, which is 10.7 miles from the intersection of Charleston and Rainbow Boulevards. Turn right (north) onto the Scenic Loop road (one-way), then drive 9.0 miles to the Pine Creek Canyon Overlook/Trailhead, which is on the right. GPS: UTM 11S 637408E 3999266N

The Hike

Follow the trail downhill to the closed dirt road that leads to the old Horace Wilson homestead site; nothing remains except the foundation. Pioneer families picked sites like this to homestead because of the water source and the cooler climate, which gave them a better chance of successfully growing crops and raising domesticated animals.

The canyon divides above the homestead site; either fork can be followed, but the left is preferable. Pine Creek was named for the unusual occurrence of ponderosa pines at this elevation in the desert; the trees thrive here because of the moisture and cooler temperatures.

Ponderosa pines are easily identified by both their bark and their needles. The bark is rough and furrowed and made up of numerous small plates that resemble the pieces of a puzzle. Young trees have dark gray bark, while on older, larger trees the bark turns orange-ish in color. Ponderosa pine needles are 5 to 7 inches long and grow in bunches of three. In a wind, the long needles give a soft sighing sound to the breeze in a ponderosa pine stand, in contrast to the harsher, more alpine sound given off by short-needled fir and spruce trees.

The microclimate supporting the tall pines is caused by the high canyon walls, which increase the amount of shade, the moisture from the Pine Creek drainage, and the cool air flowing down the canyon at night. After sunset on calm, clear nights, the ground in the high mountains rapidly cools by radiating its heat to the open sky. This in turn cools the air in contact with the earth. The cool air is heavier than warmer air and starts to flow downward, collecting in the drainages and moving toward the valleys via the canyons. This is why there is often a down canyon breeze or even a wind in desert canyons and mountain valleys after sunset. The cool air fills the valley bottoms, forming a nighttime inversion, trapping the cool, moist air under the warmer air aloft. If you hike into Pine Creek Canyon around sunrise on

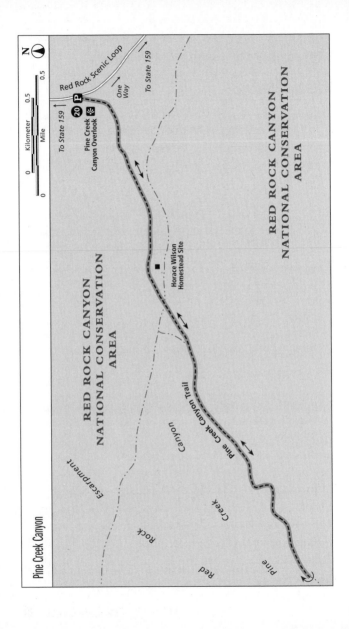

Pine Creek Canyon

a calm morning, you can feel a ten- or even twenty-degree temperature drop as you near the drainage.

Miles and Directions

0.0   Leave the Pine Creek Trailhead and Viewpoint on the Pine Creek Trail, which descends the bluff below the trailhead.

0.7   Pass the Horace Wilson homestead site, on the left.

1.2   The Pine Creek Trail enters the Mouth of Pine Creek Canyon.

1.5   Pine Creek Canyon forks; turn left onto the left fork.

2.5   Trail fades out at this approximate point; return the way you came.

5.0   Arrive back at Pine Creek Trailhead.

Clubs and Trail Groups

Friends of Nevada Wilderness
P.O. Box 9754
Reno, NV 89507
(775) 324-7667
www.nevadawilderness.org/

Las Vegas Mountaineering Club
www.lvmc.org
info@lvmc.org

Sierra Club
Toiyabe Chapter
Box 8096
Reno, NV 89507
http://nevada.sierraclub.org

The Nature Conservancy
Southern Nevada Office
1771 E. Flamingo Rd., Suite 104A
Las Vegas, NV 89119
(702) 737-8744 ext. 11
www.nature.org/wherewework/northamerica/states/
   nevada/
nevada@tnc.org

About the Author

Bruce Grubbs has been hiking, cross-country skiing, paddling, biking, and climbing in the Southwest for more than thirty years. In addition to outdoor writing and photography, he is an active charter pilot.

His other FalconGuides include these titles:
Basic Essentials: Using GPS
Best Easy Day Hikes Albuquerque
Best Easy Day Hikes Flagstaff
Best Easy Day Hikes Sedona
Best Easy Day Hikes Tucson
Best Hikes Near Phoenix
Camping Arizona
Desert Hiking Tips
Explore! Joshua Tree National Park
Explore! Mount Shasta Country
Grand Canyon National Park Pocket Guide
FalconGuide to Saguaro National Park and the Santa Catalina Mountains
Hiking Arizona
Hiking Arizona's Superstition and Mazatzal Country
Hiking Great Basin National Park
Hiking Northern Arizona
Hiking Oregon's Central Cascades
Joshua Tree National Park Pocket Guide
Mountain Biking Flagstaff and Sedona
Mountain Biking Phoenix
Mountain Biking St. George and Cedar City